NFT INVESTING 101

A BEGINNER'S GUIDE TO COLLECTIBLE DIGITAL ASSETS

Usiere Uko

...To explorers of new frontiers

CONTENTS

INTRODUCTION

I n recent years, the world of digital assets has exploded with the rise of blockchain technology. One of the most popular forms of digital assets aside from cryptocurrencies is non-fungible tokens (NFTs). NFTs are unique digital assets that represent ownership of a specific item or piece of content. They have gained tremendous popularity in the art and music world, with some NFTs selling for millions of dollars.

If you are interested in investing in NFTs but don't know where to start, "NFT Investing 101: A Beginner's Guide to Collectible Digital Assets" is the perfect book for you. This book is designed to provide a comprehensive introduction to NFTs and guide you through the process of investing in them.

The book covers everything you need to know about NFTs, including their history, how they work, and the different types of NFTs that are available. You will learn about the different marketplaces where you can buy and sell NFTs, as well as the factors that can affect their value.

The book also provides practical advice on how to invest in NFTs, including tips on how to identify valuable NFTs, how to store them securely, and how to sell them for a profit.

Whether you are a seasoned investor looking to diversify your portfolio or a beginner interested in exploring the world of digital assets, "NFT Investing 101: A Beginner's Guide to Collectible Digital Assets" is the ultimate guide to investing in NFTs.

1: WHAT ARE NFTS?

NFTs, or Non-Fungible Tokens, have become a new way for creators and collectors to buy, sell, and own digital assets. According to Wikipedia: *A non-fungible token is a unique digital identifier that cannot be copied, substituted, or subdivided, that is recorded in a blockchain, and that is used to certify ownership and authenticity*

In simple terms, an NFT is a unique digital asset that is authenticated on a blockchain, making it a one-of-a-kind item that cannot be duplicated.

What a blockchain is and how it works will be discussed in further detail in subsequent chapters.

Fungible, according to dictionary.com means *capable of being exchanged or interchanged; interchangeable.*

Hence, fungible assets are those that can be easily exchanged for (or replaced with) another asset of the same value.

For example, a dollar bill is fungible because it can be exchanged for another dollar bill of the same value. If you buy a new home appliance that turns out to be faulty, you have the option of exchanging it with the same model that works, since they have the same value.

On the other hand, a non-fungible asset is something that is unique and cannot be exchanged for something else of the same value.

For example, a painting by a famous artist is a non-fungible asset because it is unique and cannot be exchanged for another painting of the same value. There is only one Mona Lisa by Leonardo da Vinci. If it gets shredded for whatever reason, it is irreplaceable, even if you raise Leonardo from the dead.

NFTs are essentially digital versions of non-fungible assets.

One way to think of NFTs is as digital certificates of ownership. When you buy an NFT, you are buying a digital certificate that proves you own a particular asset. This asset could be a piece of art, a music file, or even a tweet.

NFTs are created using blockchain technology, which is the same technology used for cryptocurrencies like Bitcoin and Ethereum. Each NFT is verified on the blockchain, which means that it has a unique digital signature that proves its authenticity and ownership.

This digital signature is what makes NFTs valuable, as it is a proof of ownership and authenticity.

NFTs are often sold at auction, with buyers bidding against each other to own a particular asset.

Once the sale is complete, the buyer receives the NFT, which they can store in a digital wallet. NFTs are bought and sold using cryptocurrency, such as Bitcoin or Ethereum, etc. Once an NFT is purchased, it is transferred to the buyer's digital wallet, where it can be stored, traded, or sold.

Because NFTs are unique, their value is determined by supply and demand, much like traditional art or collectibles.

One of the most exciting things about NFTs is that they offer a new way for creators to monetize their digital creations. In the past, creators have struggled to monetize their digital content, as it is so easy for people to share and copy digital files.

NFTs offer a new way to create scarcity and exclusivity around digital content, which can increase its value.

For example, Beeple, a digital artist, recently sold an NFT of his artwork for a record-breaking $69 million. This sale has put NFTs in the spotlight and has made many people sit up and take notice of this new form of ownership.

Another interesting aspect of NFTs is that they are programmable, meaning that they can be designed to perform certain actions or have specific properties. For example, an NFT could be programmed to automatically pay the creator a percentage of any future sales, or it could be programmed to unlock additional content for the owner.

One potential downside of NFTs is that they have been criticized for their environmental impact. Blockchain technology uses a lot of energy, and the process of creating and selling NFTs can be quite energy-intensive.

However, some companies and individuals are working on solutions to reduce the environmental impact of blockchain technology.

NFTs are a new and exciting way for creators and collectors to buy, sell, and own digital assets. They offer a unique way to monetize digital content and for buyers to own a piece of digital history while providing a new avenue for investment.

While the NFT market is still relatively new and there are some concerns about its environmental impact and speculative nature, it is clear that NFTs are here to stay and will continue to shape the future of digital ownership and investment, and the way we think about the value of digital content.

2: BRIEF HISTORY OF NFTS

While NFTs have only recently gained mainstream attention, the concept has been around for several years.

In 2012, Meni Rosenfield introduced the 'Colored Coins' concept for the Bitcoin blockchain, which aimed to represent and manage real-world assets on the blockchain to prove ownership. However, the limitations of Bitcoin prevented the realization of this concept, which paved the way for the invention of NFTs.

On May 3rd, 2014, Kevin McCoy created the first-known NFT 'Quantum' on the Namecoin blockchain. This digital artwork featured a pixelated octagon that changed color and pulsated in a hypnotic manner similar to an octopus.

Numerous experiments and developments took place after the creation of 'Quantum', with platforms built on top of the Bitcoin blockchain. The Ethereum blockchain also emerged as a significant player in the NFT market.

Ethereum is a decentralized blockchain platform that allows for the creation of smart contracts, which are self-executing contracts with the terms of the agreement between buyer and seller being directly written into lines of code.

Counterparty, a Bitcoin 2.0 platform, allowed for the creation of digital assets and gained popularity. Spells of Genesis followed Counterparty and started issuing in-game assets.

However, it wasn't until the launch of the Ethereum blockchain in 2015 that the concept of NFTs really took off.

One of the first NFT projects on Ethereum was CryptoKitties, a blockchain-based game where users could breed and trade unique digital cats. The game became so popular that it caused congestion on the Ethereum network, leading to delays and higher transaction fees. Despite these issues, CryptoKitties demonstrated the potential for NFTs to create unique and valuable digital assets.

In 2017, a project called CryptoKitties was launched on the Ethereum blockchain, which allowed users to buy, sell, and breed digital cats as collectibles. Each cat was represented as a unique NFT, meaning that no two cats were exactly alike and each had its own specific value and ownership.

This project helped to popularize the idea of NFTs as a means of creating and selling unique digital assets on the blockchain. Since then, NFTs have been used to represent a wide variety of digital content, such as artwork, music, videos, and even tweets.

In early 2021, the market for NFTs exploded, with some digital assets selling for millions of dollars. This surge in popularity has led to increased interest and investment in the development of NFT technology and platforms.

While there are still many questions about the long-term viability and use cases for NFTs, they represent a potentially groundbreaking development in the world of digital ownership and value exchange.

3: POTENTIAL APPLICATIONS OF NFTS

N on-fungible tokens (NFTs) have gained widespread attention due to their unique digital ownership capabilities. While they are currently most commonly associated with digital artwork, NFTs have the potential for a wide range of applications across industries.

Here are some of the potential applications of NFTs:

ART AND COLLECTIBLES

NFTs have already become popular in the art world, with digital art pieces selling for millions of dollars. NFTs provide a new way for artists to monetize their work, as they can sell digital art directly to collectors without the need for intermediaries. NFTs also allow for the creation of unique and rare collectibles, such as rare trading cards and limited-edition merchandise.

MUSIC

NFTs can also be used in the music and entertainment industry, allowing artists and musicians to monetize their work in new and innovative ways. For example, musicians can sell limited-edition vinyl records or concert tickets as NFTs, providing fans with a unique and collectible item.

GAMING

NFTs can be used to represent unique in-game assets, such as weapons, skins, and characters. Players can own and trade these assets, creating a new level of engagement and value in the gaming world.

REAL ESTATE AND VIRTUAL WORLDS

NFTs can also be used to represent ownership of physical assets, such as real estate or virtual property in video games and virtual worlds (Metaverse, etc.). For example, an NFT could represent ownership of a plot of land in a virtual world, allowing players to buy, sell, and trade virtual property.

IDENTITY AND AUTHENTICATION

NFTs can also be used to verify identity and authentication, providing a secure and transparent way to store and verify personal information. For example, NFTs could be used to store and verify academic credentials or professional certifications, reducing the risk of fraud and increasing trust in the verification process.

TICKETING

NFTs can be used to represent unique event tickets, reducing the risk of fraud and scalping. This can create a more secure and efficient ticketing process for both event organizers and attendees.

AUTHENTICATION OF PRODUCTS

NFTs provide a way to verify the authenticity of a product before purchase. The use of blockchain technology allows for permanent storage of information about the product, enabling the ability to verify rarity and authenticity. This verification system is not limited to digital assets, as it may soon be extended to physical products as well.

Additionally, NFTs can also serve as a means of recording information about the manufacturing process, thus guaranteeing that everything is fair trade.

INTELLECTUAL PROPERTY AND PATENTS

Traditional tools for protecting intellectual property rights, such as trademarks and copyrights, do not provide a means for users to demonstrate ownership of specific pieces of content. In contrast, NFT tokens allow users to establish and verify their ownership of digital assets through a publicly accessible, immutable record of transactions. This record, which includes timestamps and the complete history of the asset, can be used to demonstrate original creation or ownership at any time.

NFTs can also be used to protect and certify ownership of innovations or inventions, much like patents. By providing a verifiable and transparent record of transactions related to patents, NFTs can create a public ledger that serves as a reliable source of information for patent verification.

ACADEMIC CREDENTIALS

NFTs offer a promising solution for representing academic credentials in a secure and tamper-proof manner. They provide an effective means for verifying key information, such as attendance records, degrees earned, and other relevant data, which is then stored on an immutable NFT chain, impervious to any potential hacking or tampering.

By issuing tokens for each course completed, NFTs can create permanent records for the courses taken and the corresponding credentials earned, leveraging smart contract verification systems for added security and authenticity. This makes NFTs a reliable and transparent way to demonstrate academic achievements, providing a trusted and accessible source of information for potential employers or other interested parties.

SUPPLY CHAIN MANAGEMENT

NFTs can be used in Supply Chain Management to help verify the authenticity and provenance of goods throughout the supply chain. NFTs can be used to track and trace the movement of goods throughout the supply chain. Each NFT can represent a specific item, and its unique digital signature can be used to verify its authenticity and ownership at every stage of the supply chain.

NFTs can be used to verify the origin and authenticity of goods. By attaching an NFT to a product at the point of origin, the entire supply chain can be tracked to ensure that the product is genuine and has not been tampered with. NFTs can be used to verify the quality of goods. For example, an NFT can be attached to a batch of goods to ensure that they meet certain quality standards. This can help prevent the distribution of counterfeit or defective products.

NFTs can be used as collateral for supply chain financing. By attaching an NFT to a product, the lender can verify its authenticity and value, which can help reduce the risk of fraud and increase the availability of financing for suppliers.

***

Potential applications of NFTs are virtually limitless. NFTs have the potential to revolutionize the way we own and trade digital and real-world assets across various industries, including supply chains, etc. As the technology develops, we can expect to see new and innovative applications of NFTs emerge.

4: TYPES OF NFTS

NFTs can take many forms, and there are a variety of different types of NFTs that are available to collectors and investors. In this article, we will explore some of the most common types of NFTs, including art, gaming items, sports memorabilia, and more.

ART NFTs

Art NFTs are some of the most well-known and popular types of NFTs. They allow artists to create unique, digital works of art that can be bought and sold like traditional artwork. Here are some of the ways in which art NFTs are being used:

1. Selling Original Art

Artists can create digital art and sell it as a unique, one-of-a-kind NFT. This allows them to retain ownership of the original artwork while allowing buyers to own a unique piece of digital art.

2. Limited Edition Prints

Artists can create limited edition prints of their artwork and sell them as NFTs. These NFTs can represent the ownership of a specific edition of the artwork, making them highly valuable to collectors.

3. Royalties and Resale Rights

NFTs can be programmed to include a royalty or resale right for the artist. This means that every time the NFT is sold or resold, the artist receives a percentage of the sale.

4. Curated Collections

NFT platforms can curate collections of digital art based on a theme or style. These collections can be sold as individual NFTs or as a collection, creating a new way for artists to showcase and sell their work.

5. Interactive Art

NFTs can be used to create interactive art that changes over time or in response to user input. This creates a new level of engagement for buyers and collectors, making the art more valuable and desirable.

6. Virtual Galleries

NFT platforms can create virtual galleries where buyers can view and purchase digital art. This creates a new way for artists to showcase their work and reach a global audience.

PHOTOGRAPHY NFTs

Photography is one of the most popular art forms that can be monetized using NFTs. Non-fungible tokens (NFTs) allow photographers to sell their digital photographs as unique, one-of-a-kind assets that cannot be replicated or duplicated. Here are some of the ways in which photography NFTs are being used:

1. Selling Original Photographs

Photographers can mint and sell their original digital photographs as NFTs. These NFTs represent the ownership and authenticity of the original photograph and can be sold to collectors or buyers who want to own a unique piece of digital art.

2. Limited Edition Prints

Photographers can create limited edition prints of their photographs and sell them as NFTs. These NFTs can represent the ownership of a specific edition of a photograph, making them highly valuable to collectors.

3. Royalties and Resale Rights

NFTs can be programmed to include a royalty or resale right for the photographer. This means that every time the NFT is sold or resold, the photographer receives a percentage of the sale.

4. Curated Collections

NFT platforms can curate collections of photographs based on a theme or style. These collections can be sold as individual NFTs or as a collection, creating a new way for photographers to showcase and sell their work.

5. Personalized Content

Photographers can offer personalized content, such as portraits or event photography, as NFTs. Buyers can commission the photographer to create a unique piece of art that they own as an NFT.

AVATARS NFTs

Non-fungible tokens (NFTs) have also created a new market for digital avatars, allowing users to create and customize their own unique online identities. Here are some of the ways in which avatar NFTs are being used:

1. Personalized Avatars

Users can create and customize their own avatars as NFTs, allowing them to own and control their online identities.

2. Gaming Avatars

NFTs are being used in gaming as a way to represent in-game characters and items. Users can buy, sell, and trade these NFTs as they progress through the game.

3. Social Media

NFTs are being used on social media platforms as a way to represent users' profiles and identities. This creates a new level of ownership and control over their online presence.

4. Virtual Reality

NFTs can be used to represent avatars in virtual reality environments, allowing users to own and control their virtual selves.

5. Collectibles

Avatar NFTs can be collected and traded, creating a new market for unique and valuable digital assets.

6. Celebrity Avatars

Celebrities can create their own avatars as NFTs, allowing fans to own a unique piece of digital memorabilia.

GAMING NFTs

Gaming NFTs are another popular type of NFT that allows gamers to buy and sell unique in-game items, characters, and other virtual assets. These NFTs can be used in various games and are often used to enhance the gaming experience for players.

For example, in the popular blockchain game Axie Infinity, players can buy and sell NFTs that represent different Axies, which are cute, digital creatures that players can collect, breed, and battle with.

These NFTs can be traded on various marketplaces and can be worth thousands of dollars, making them a valuable investment for players and collectors alike. Here are some of the ways in which gaming NFTs are being used:

1. In-game items

NFTs can be used to represent rare or unique in-game items such as weapons, armor, skins, and other accessories. These items can be sold or traded on various marketplaces for real-world currency.

2. Virtual real estate

NFTs can represent ownership of virtual real estate within a game world. This can include virtual buildings, land, or even entire planets in some games.

3. Character ownership

NFTs can be used to represent ownership of specific characters or avatars within a game. This can give players a sense of ownership and pride in their virtual identity.

4. Collectibles

NFTs can be used to create limited-edition or rare collectibles within a game. These collectibles can be valuable to players who are interested in building a unique collection.

5. Rewards and achievements

NFTs can be used to represent rewards or achievements earned by players within a game. For example, a player who completes a particularly difficult level or challenge may be rewarded with an NFT that represents their accomplishment.

SPORTS NFTs

Sports NFTs, or non-fungible tokens, are digital assets that represent ownership or proof of authenticity of sports-related collectibles, events, or memorabilia. These NFTs use blockchain technology to create unique and verifiable digital assets that cannot be replicated.

Sports NFTs have gained popularity in recent years as they offer a new way for sports fans to collect and invest in rare and unique sports memorabilia. NFTs can be used to represent ownership of sports cards, game-worn jerseys, autographed items, and even ownership of sports teams.

Sports NFTs also offer new revenue streams for sports organizations and athletes. Teams and leagues can create limited-edition NFTs for special events or moments, and athletes can sell NFTs to fans as a way to monetize their personal brands and fan engagement. Here are some of the ways in which sports NFTs are being used:

1. Collectibles

NFTs can be used to represent ownership of rare or unique sports collectibles such as game-worn jerseys, autographed items, and trading cards. These items can be sold or traded on various marketplaces for real-world currency.

2. Virtual experiences

NFTs can be used to provide fans with virtual experiences such as access to exclusive events, meet and greets with athletes, or behind-the-scenes content.

3. Fan engagement

NFTs can be used to engage fans and create a sense of community. For example, a sports team can create limited-edition NFTs for their fans, which can be used to access exclusive content, merchandise, or even discounted tickets.

4. Team ownership

NFTs can be used to represent ownership of sports teams. Fans can purchase NFTs that give them a stake in the team, which can provide them with voting rights or a share of team revenue.

5. Historic moments

NFTs can be used to represent ownership of historic sports moments such as a game-winning shot or a record-breaking performance. These NFTs can be valuable to collectors who are interested in owning a piece of sports history.

VIRTUAL REAL ESTATE NFTs

Virtual real estate NFTs (Non-Fungible Tokens) are digital assets that represent ownership of virtual land or property in a digital world or metaverse. These NFTs are unique and cannot be replicated, making them valuable for collectors and investors.

Virtual real estate NFTs are becoming increasingly popular as virtual worlds and metaverses continue to gain traction. These digital spaces offer unique experiences and opportunities for social interaction, gaming, and even commerce. Owners of virtual real estate NFTs can potentially earn income through renting or selling their virtual property, and these NFTs can also appreciate in value based on market demand.

Some popular virtual worlds and metaverses where virtual real estate NFTs are traded include Decentraland, The Sandbox, Somnium Space, and Cryptovoxels. These platforms allow users to buy, sell, and develop virtual real estate using cryptocurrency and blockchain technology. Here are some of the ways in which sports NFTs are being used:

1. Gaming

Virtual Real Estate NFTs are used in gaming to represent land or property within a virtual world or game. For example, players can own virtual real estate within games like Decentraland, The Sandbox, and Axie Infinity.

2. Virtual Events

NFTs can be used to represent virtual spaces where events can be hosted, such as conferences, concerts, and exhibitions.

3. Advertising

Virtual Real Estate NFTs can be used for advertising purposes, allowing brands to own virtual properties where they can showcase their products and services within virtual worlds.

4. Investment

Virtual Real Estate NFTs can be bought and sold like physical real estate, with their value depending on location, demand, and other factors. Some investors are purchasing virtual real estate NFTs as a long-term investment.

5. Virtual Real Estate Development

Developers can use virtual real estate NFTs to create and sell virtual properties and structures within virtual worlds, like buildings, bridges, and landmarks.

6. Social Networks

Virtual Real Estate NFTs can be used to create social networks within virtual worlds, where users can buy and own virtual properties, interact with other users, and build communities.

COLLECTIBLE NFTs

Collectible NFTs are a type of NFT that allows collectors to buy and sell unique, digital collectibles that are often tied to popular franchises or brands. These collectibles can take many forms, including digital trading cards, action figures, and even virtual pets. Here are some ways in which Collectible NFTs are being used:

1. Art

Collectible NFTs are commonly used to represent digital artwork, which can be bought and sold on blockchain marketplaces. The ownership of the digital asset is verified through the blockchain, making it unique and valuable.

2. Sports

Collectible NFTs are used in the sports world to represent trading cards or other memorabilia items. For example, NBA Top Shot is a popular platform where users can buy and sell NFTs representing basketball highlights.

3. Gaming

Collectible NFTs are also used in the gaming industry to represent in-game items, such as weapons, skins, or rare items. These NFTs can be bought and sold on blockchain marketplaces, allowing players to own unique and valuable assets within the game.

4. Music

Collectible NFTs are used in the music industry to represent digital music and other unique assets, such as concert tickets or backstage passes. These NFTs can be bought and sold on blockchain marketplaces, allowing fans to own unique and valuable assets related to their favorite artists.

5. Fashion

Collectible NFTs can be used to represent limited-edition or rare fashion items, such as sneakers or designer clothing. The ownership of these items can be verified through the blockchain, making them unique and valuable.

VIRTUAL FASHION NFTs

Virtual fashion NFTs are a newer type of NFT that has been gaining popularity in the world of fashion and entertainment. These NFTs allow creators to design unique, digital fashion items that can be bought and sold on various blockchain platforms. Virtual fashion NFTs can take many forms, including digital clothing, accessories, and even makeup.

One of the most notable examples of virtual fashion NFTs is The Fabricant, a digital fashion house that creates high-end, digital clothing and accessories that can be bought and sold as NFTs. The Fabricant has worked with various luxury brands and celebrities, and their NFTs have sold for thousands of dollars at auctions and on various marketplaces. Here are some ways in which Virtual Fashion NFTs are being used:

1. Fashion Shows

Virtual Fashion NFTs are used to showcase new collections and designs in virtual fashion shows. Designers can create unique and exclusive pieces of virtual clothing and sell them as NFTs on blockchain marketplaces.

2. Social Media

Virtual Fashion NFTs are used to create unique and eye-catching content for social media platforms, such as Instagram, TikTok, and Twitter. Influencers can wear and showcase virtual clothing and accessories, generating interest and hype around the NFTs.

3. Gaming

Virtual Fashion NFTs are used in gaming to represent virtual clothing and accessories that can be bought and sold on blockchain marketplaces. Players can customize their avatars with unique and exclusive virtual fashion items, making their characters stand out from the crowd.

4. Metaverse

Virtual Fashion NFTs are used to represent unique and exclusive clothing and accessories within the metaverse. Users can buy and sell virtual fashion items, creating a new digital economy within the virtual world.

5. Art

Virtual Fashion NFTs can be considered digital art, representing unique and exclusive pieces of virtual clothing and accessories. These NFTs can be bought and sold on blockchain marketplaces, allowing collectors to own unique and valuable pieces of digital art.

MUSIC NFTs

Music NFTs are a type of NFT that allows musicians and artists to sell unique, digital music files that can be bought and sold on blockchain platforms. These NFTs can take many forms, including full albums, individual songs, and even exclusive access to live performances and events.

One notable example of a music NFT is Grimes' "WarNymph" digital art and music collection, which was released in February 2021. The collection includes a variety of digital art pieces and music tracks, and the NFTs were sold on Nifty Gateway for a total of nearly $6 million. Here are some ways in which Music NFTs are being used:

1. Royalties

Music NFTs are used to represent ownership of music royalties.

The owner of the NFT can receive a share of the revenue generated from the music, such as streaming royalties, mechanical royalties, and performance royalties.

2. Collectibles

Music NFTs are used as collectibles, representing unique and exclusive pieces of music-related content. For example, a musician can create an NFT that represents a rare demo version of a song or an autographed album cover.

3. Fan engagement

Music NFTs are used to engage with fans, offering unique and exclusive content and experiences to those who own the NFT. For example, a musician can offer exclusive backstage passes or meet and greet sessions to fans who own their NFT.

4. Crowdfunding

Music NFTs are used for crowdfunding campaigns, allowing fans to invest in new music projects and receive exclusive rewards and experiences in return. The ownership of the NFT can represent a share of the revenue generated from the project.

5. Ticketing

Music NFTs are used for ticketing and event access, allowing fans to own an NFT that represents their entry to a concert, festival, or other music event. The ownership of the NFT can be verified through the blockchain, ensuring secure and efficient ticketing.

Art NFTs remain the most popular and widely traded NFTs, but the other types are rapidly gaining popularity.

With the continued growth of blockchain technology and the increasing adoption of NFTs by artists, musicians, athletes, and collectors, it is clear that NFTs will continue to shape the future of the digital art market and beyond. As the technology and market for NFTs continue to evolve, it will be interesting to see what new types of NFTs emerge and how they are used to revolutionize the digital asset industry.

5: HOW NFTS WORK

I n this chapter, we will explore the ins and outs of NFTs, how they are created, and what makes them unique.

HOW ARE NFTs CREATED?

NFTs are typically created using a process called "minting," which involves creating a new digital asset and assigning it a unique identifier on the blockchain.

This identifier serves as proof of ownership and authenticity, and is recorded on the blockchain in a way that cannot be altered or deleted.

The process of minting an NFT typically involves the following steps:

1. Choose a platform

There are several platforms that allow users to create and sell NFTs, including OpenSea, Rarible, and SuperRare. Each platform has its own requirements and fees, so it's important to do your research before choosing one.

2. Create your asset

This could be a piece of artwork, a tweet, or any other type of digital content that you want to represent as an NFT.

3. Upload your asset

Once you have created your asset, you will need to upload it to the platform you have chosen. This will typically involve uploading a digital file, such as a JPEG or MP3. Then a smart contract is created.

The smart contract contains the details of the NFT, including its ownership, metadata, and any rules or conditions associated with it.

4. Mint your NFT

After uploading your asset, you will be prompted to mint your NFT. This involves assigning a unique identifier, or token, to your asset on the blockchain. This token serves as a digital certificate of ownership and authenticity, and cannot be duplicated or transferred without the owner's consent. The token is what makes the NFT non-fungible, as it cannot be exchanged for another token or asset of equal value.

5. Set your price

Once your NFT has been minted, you can set a price for it. This price is usually denominated in cryptocurrency, such as Ethereum, and can vary widely depending on the perceived value of the asset.

6. Market and sell your NFT

Finally, you will need to market and sell your NFT to potential buyers. This can be done through social media, online marketplaces, or by working with a broker or auction house.

WHAT MAKES NFTs UNIQUE?

So what makes NFTs different from other types of digital assets? There are several key features that make NFTs unique:

1. Scarcity

NFTs are designed to be scarce, meaning there is a limited supply of each asset. This scarcity is what gives NFTs their value, as collectors are willing to pay a premium for unique and rare items.

2. Authenticity

NFTs are also designed to be authentic, meaning they serve as a digital certificate of ownership and authenticity. This is especially important for digital assets, which can be easily copied or duplicated without proper safeguards in place.

3. Interoperability

NFTs are designed to be interoperable, meaning they can be exchanged or used across different platforms and applications. This allows for greater flexibility and ease of use, as NFTs can be used for a wide range of purposes, from gaming to art to social media.

4. Transparency

NFTs are also designed to be transparent, meaning that all transactions are recorded on the blockchain and can be easily traced and verified. This transparency is especially important for the art and collectibles market, where authenticity and provenance are key considerations.

5. Programmability

NFTs can be programmed with smart contracts, which can automate certain actions and enable complex transactions. For example, an NFT can be programmed to pay out royalties to the original creator every time it is sold.

6: BLOCKCHAIN TECHNOLOGY AND NFTS

Blockchain technology has been making waves across industries since its inception in 2008. Its most popular implementation, Bitcoin, quickly caught the attention of the financial world, but the potential uses of blockchain technology extend far beyond currency.

One of the most exciting developments in recent years is the emergence of non-fungible tokens (NFTs), which use blockchain technology to represent unique digital assets. In this chapter, we will explore how blockchain technology and NFTs are changing the digital landscape.

WHAT IS BLOCKCHAIN TECHNOLOGY?

Blockchain technology is a decentralized and distributed digital ledger that is used to record transactions across multiple computers or nodes. Each block in the chain contains a timestamp and a unique cryptographic code, which makes it virtually impossible to alter or manipulate the data in the ledger.

Here are some key features of blockchain technology:

1. Decentralization

Blockchain technology is decentralized, which means that there is no central authority or entity that controls the ledger. Instead, the ledger is distributed across a network of nodes, which makes it more resilient and secure.

2. Transparency

Because the blockchain ledger is public and transparent, anyone can view the transactions and verify their authenticity. This helps to increase trust and accountability in the system.

3. Security

Blockchain technology uses cryptography to secure the data in the ledger. Each block in the chain contains a unique cryptographic code that is linked to the previous block, which makes it virtually impossible to alter or tamper with the data in the ledger.

4. Immutability

Once a block has been added to the blockchain, it cannot be changed or deleted. This means that the data in the blockchain is immutable and provides a tamper-proof record of transactions.

NFTs (non-fungible tokens) use blockchain technology to provide a secure and transparent way to verify ownership and provenance of digital assets.

When an NFT is created, a unique digital signature is added to the blockchain ledger, which serves as proof of ownership and authenticity. This digital signature is stored on every node in the network, which makes it virtually impossible to alter or manipulate.

Whenever an NFT is sold or transferred, the transaction is recorded on the blockchain ledger, which allows anyone to view the history of ownership and provenance of the asset. This makes it easy to verify the authenticity of the asset and provides a transparent record of its ownership.

By using blockchain technology, NFTs provide a secure and transparent way to represent, verify, and exchange digital assets, such as artwork, music, and videos. They can be bought and sold on various online marketplaces, and their value is determined by market demand and the uniqueness of the underlying asset.

7: ADVANTAGES AND DISADVANTAGES OF NFTS

I n this chapter, we will examine the advantages and disadvantages of NFTs, exploring both sides of the coin.

ADVANTAGES OF NFTS

Authenticity and provenance

One of the main advantages of NFTs is that they allow creators to establish the authenticity and provenance of their digital assets. By creating an NFT, an artist can prove that they are the original creator of a piece of digital art, music, or other digital asset. This is particularly valuable in a world where digital assets can be easily copied and distributed without the creators receiving any credit or compensation.

Increased revenue for creators

Another advantage of NFTs is that they offer creators a new way to monetize their work. By creating an NFT, artists can sell their work directly to collectors, without having to go through traditional intermediaries like galleries or auction houses. This can lead to increased revenue for artists, as they can set their own prices and receive a larger share of the profits from their sales.

Accessibility

NFTs also offer a new level of accessibility to art and other digital assets. Unlike traditional art, which is often locked up in museums or private collections, NFTs can be easily shared and viewed by anyone with an internet connection. This can lead to a democratization of the art world, as more people are able to engage with and appreciate art that they might not otherwise have had access to.

Immutable ownership

NFTs are stored on a blockchain, which means that they are immutable and cannot be altered or deleted. This provides a level of security and permanence to owners of NFTs, as they can be confident that their ownership of a particular asset is indisputable. This is particularly valuable in a world where digital assets can be easily copied or stolen.

DISADVANTAGES OF NFTs

Environmental impact

One of the main criticisms of NFTs is their environmental impact. The process of creating and selling NFTs requires a significant amount of energy, which can contribute to climate change. This is because most NFTs are created using the Ethereum blockchain, which uses a proof-of-work consensus algorithm that requires a large amount of computing power. This has led to concerns about the carbon footprint of NFTs, and calls for alternative blockchain technologies that are more energy-efficient.

Speculation and volatility

Another disadvantage of NFTs is that they can be highly speculative and volatile. Because NFTs are a relatively new asset class, their value can fluctuate wildly based on market demand and hype. This can lead to a bubble-like situation, where NFTs are bought and sold at inflated prices, only to crash in value when the market cools off. This can be particularly harmful to artists and collectors who invest heavily in NFTs, as they may lose a significant amount of money if the market crashes.

Inequality and elitism

NFTs have also been criticized for exacerbating existing inequalities in the art world. Because NFTs are often sold for large sums of money, they can be seen as elitist and exclusive, catering only to wealthy collectors. This can be especially troubling for emerging artists, who may not have the financial resources or connections to break into the NFT market. Additionally, the high prices of NFTs can make it difficult for ordinary people to afford to buy them, which can create a divide between those who can afford to own NFTs and those who cannot.

Lack of regulation

Another concern with NFTs is the lack of regulation in the market. Because NFTs are a relatively new asset class, there are few regulations in place to protect investors and buyers. This can lead to fraudulent practices and scams, where individuals create fake NFTs or misrepresent the value of their NFTs in order to profit off of unsuspecting buyers.

Technical limitations

Finally, there are technical limitations to NFTs that can limit their usefulness in certain applications. For example, NFTs are currently limited to storing metadata and ownership information, which means that they may not be suitable for all types of digital assets. Additionally, NFTs may not be compatible with certain blockchain technologies or platforms, which can limit their reach and utility.

***

Ultimately, the future of NFTs will depend on how the market and technology develop, as well as how regulators respond to the growing popularity of NFTs.

As with any emerging technology or asset class, it is important to approach NFTs with caution and to carefully consider both the potential benefits and risks before investing.

8: POPULAR NFT MARKETPLACES

T here are several popular NFT marketplaces where users can buy, sell, and trade digital assets. Here are some of the most popular ones:

1. OPENSEA

OpenSea is one of the largest and most popular NFT marketplaces, allowing users to buy, sell, and discover a wide range of digital assets, including art, gaming items, collectibles, and more. The platform supports a variety of blockchain networks, including Ethereum, Polygon, and others.

One of the key features of OpenSea is its user-friendly interface, which makes it easy for both new and experienced users to navigate and use the platform. It also offers a range of advanced features, such as the ability to create custom collections, set royalties, and enable auctions.

OpenSea has a large and active community of users, which helps to drive demand and interest in NFTs on the platform. It also features a "Discover" section, which allows users to explore new and trending NFT collections and artists.

Another important feature of OpenSea is its support for gas-free trading, which enables users to buy and sell NFTs without paying transaction fees. This is achieved through the use of layer-two solutions, such as Polygon, which offer faster and cheaper transactions compared to the Ethereum network.

2. NIFTY GATEWAY

Nifty Gateway is a popular NFT marketplace that was acquired by the Winklevoss twins' cryptocurrency exchange Gemini in 2019. The platform allows users to buy, sell, and discover a variety of digital assets, including artwork, music, and other collectibles.

One of the key features of Nifty Gateway is its focus on exclusive drops and limited-edition releases, which creates a sense of scarcity and exclusivity for buyers. The platform partners with high-profile artists and celebrities to create unique and highly sought-after NFT collections.

Nifty Gateway also features a user-friendly interface and a range of advanced features, such as the ability to set royalties and enable auctions. The platform supports both Ethereum and Flow blockchains, which allows for a wider range of digital assets to be traded.

Another important feature of Nifty Gateway is its integration with Gemini's cryptocurrency exchange, which allows for seamless purchasing and trading of NFTs using fiat currency. This makes it easy for users to enter and exit the NFT market without the need for a cryptocurrency wallet.

3. SUPERRARE

SuperRare is a curated NFT marketplace that specializes in showcasing and selling high-quality, unique digital artworks. The platform focuses on supporting artists and creators and helping them to monetize their works through the sale of NFTs.

One of the key features of SuperRare is its strict curation process, which ensures that only high-quality, original works are featured on the platform. This creates a sense of exclusivity and quality for buyers and helps to promote the value of the NFTs sold on the platform.

SuperRare also features a unique auction system, which allows for bidding to take place in either cryptocurrency or fiat currency. This opens up the platform to a wider range of potential buyers, including those who may not be familiar with cryptocurrency.

Another important feature of SuperRare is its focus on community and engagement. The platform has a strong social media presence and encourages users to interact with each other and with the artists whose works are featured on the platform. This creates a sense of excitement and exclusivity for buyers and helps to build a loyal user base.

SuperRare features a transparent and secure provenance system, which provides a secure and transparent record of ownership for each NFT. This helps to prevent fraud and ensures that buyers can have confidence in the authenticity of the NFTs they purchase.

4. RARIBLE

Rarible is an open marketplace for buying, selling, and discovering a wide range of NFTs, including digital art, collectibles, and gaming items. The platform is built on the Ethereum blockchain and allows users to create and sell their own NFTs.

One of the key features of Rarible is its easy-to-use platform, which allows users to create and sell their own NFTs without requiring any technical expertise. This makes it easy for artists, creators, and collectors to participate in the NFT market and monetize their digital assets.

Rarible also features a reputation system, which allows users to build trust and establish a reputation within the platform's community. This helps to promote fair and transparent trading practices and encourages users to engage with each other.

Another important feature of Rarible is its support for community-driven initiatives, such as governance and tokenization. The platform allows users to participate in the governance of the platform through a community-driven decision-making process, and it also allows for the creation and trading of community-specific tokens.

5. FOUNDATION

Foundation is a curated NFT marketplace that primarily focuses on supporting emerging and established digital artists and creators. It is a platform where artists can showcase and sell their unique digital creations, including digital art, music, and other creative works. Foundation has a strict curation process, and not all submissions are accepted, ensuring that only the highest quality and most innovative works are showcased on the platform.

One of the unique features of Foundation is the ability for creators to offer "unlimited editions" of their NFTs, which means that they can sell as many copies of their digital work as they want. This is different from the traditional model of selling limited edition physical artworks.

Another key feature of Foundation is its bidding system, which allows buyers to bid on NFTs and compete with each other for ownership of a particular work. This creates a sense of excitement and exclusivity for buyers, as well as potentially increasing the value of the NFT.

Foundation also offers a feature called "Creator Royalties," which enables artists to earn a percentage of future sales of their NFTs. This allows artists to continue to benefit from the success of their work even after it has been sold.

6. KNOWNORIGIN

KnownOrigin is a curated NFT marketplace that primarily focuses on supporting and promoting digital artists and creators. It is a platform where artists can showcase and sell their unique digital creations, including digital art, music, and other creative works. The platform has a strict curation process, ensuring that only high-quality and original works are featured on the platform.

One of the key features of KnownOrigin is its focus on community and engagement. The platform has a strong social media presence and encourages users to interact with each other and with the artists whose works are featured on the platform. This creates a sense of excitement and exclusivity for buyers and helps to build a loyal user base.

KnownOrigin also features a "Dutch Auction" system, which allows for a fair and transparent pricing mechanism for NFTs. This system involves gradually lowering the price of an NFT over time until a buyer is found. This incentivizes buyers to act quickly and helps to ensure that NFTs are sold at fair market value.

Another feature of KnownOrigin is its "Provenance" system, which provides a secure and transparent record of ownership for each NFT. This helps to prevent fraud and ensures that buyers can have confidence in the authenticity of the NFTs they purchase.

7. ATOMICMARKET

AtomicMarket is a decentralized NFT marketplace that operates on the WAX blockchain. It allows users to buy, sell, and trade digital assets, including NFTs, on the blockchain. AtomicMarket provides a user-friendly interface that enables users to easily navigate the platform and discover a wide range of digital assets, from gaming items to artwork and collectibles.

One of the benefits of using AtomicMarket is that it offers a low transaction fee compared to other NFT marketplaces. This is because WAX blockchain uses a delegated proof of stake (DPoS) consensus algorithm, which enables high transaction throughput and fast confirmation times, making it a popular choice for NFT marketplaces.

AtomicMarket also offers a feature called "AtomicAssets" which allows users to create their own NFTs easily. This feature provides a user-friendly interface for creating, minting, and managing NFTs on the WAX blockchain.

8. BINANCE NFT MARKETPLACE

Binance NFT Marketplace is a popular platform for buying and selling NFTs that is powered by the Binance Smart Chain. It offers a wide range of digital assets, including artwork, gaming items, music, sports collectibles, and more. The marketplace also features collections from a variety of well-known artists, celebrities, and brands.

One of the key benefits of using Binance NFT Marketplace is that it allows for easy conversion between cryptocurrencies and fiat currencies. This is because the platform is integrated with Binance's centralized exchange, which enables users to use a wide range of cryptocurrencies to purchase NFTs. Additionally, Binance NFT Marketplace has low transaction fees, making it an affordable choice for buying and selling NFTs.

Another feature of Binance NFT Marketplace is the ability for creators to set royalty rates for their NFTs. This means that they can earn a percentage of future sales of their NFTs, even if they are resold on secondary markets.

Binance NFT Marketplace also features a "Mystery Box" feature, which allows users to purchase a box containing a random assortment of NFTs from a particular collection. This creates a sense of excitement and exclusivity for buyers, as they do not know exactly what they will receive.

9. BAKERYSWAP

BakerySwap is a decentralized NFT marketplace that operates on the Binance Smart Chain. It allows users to buy, sell, and trade digital assets, including NFTs, on the blockchain. The platform features a wide range of digital assets, including artwork, music, and gaming items.

One of the unique features of BakerySwap is its integration with decentralized finance (DeFi) protocols. This allows users to earn yield on their NFT holdings, which means that they can earn a return on their investment even while their NFTs are not being actively traded.

BakerySwap also features a "Liquidity Bakery" feature, which allows users to stake their NFTs and earn rewards in return. This incentivizes users to hold onto their NFTs for longer periods of time, rather than simply buying and selling them for short-term gains.

Another key feature of BakerySwap is its "NFT Farming" feature, which enables users to earn NFTs as rewards for providing liquidity to certain NFT pools. This creates a sense of community and engagement for users, as they can earn rewards while also contributing to the liquidity of the platform.

10. HIC ET NUNC

Hic et Nunc is a popular NFT marketplace that is built on the Tezos blockchain. The platform is designed to be fast, cheap, and accessible, with a focus on supporting the creative community and promoting the adoption of blockchain technology.

One of the key features of Hic et Nunc is its low fees and fast transaction times. This makes it easy for artists and collectors to participate in the NFT market without incurring high costs or experiencing long wait times for transactions to be processed.

Another important feature of Hic et Nunc is its commitment to open-source technology and community-driven development. The platform is built on open-source software and encourages community members to contribute to its development and improvement.

Hic et Nunc also features a unique tokenization system, which allows for the creation and trading of fractional NFTs. This enables users to invest in a portion of an artwork or collectible, rather than having to purchase the entire NFT.

11. AXIE INFINITY

Axie Infinity is a blockchain-based game that uses non-fungible tokens (NFTs) as in-game assets. The game is set in a world called Lunacia, where players can collect, breed, and battle creatures called Axies.

The Axie Infinity NFT Marketplace is a platform where players can buy, sell, and trade their Axies and other in-game assets using cryptocurrencies such as Ether (ETH) and Axie Infinity Shards (AXS). The marketplace is decentralized and built on the Ethereum blockchain, which means that all transactions are recorded on the blockchain and can be verified by anyone.

Axies are unique and rare NFTs that have different attributes, such as body type, parts, and abilities, which determine their value and usefulness in battles. The marketplace allows players to set their own prices for their Axies and other in-game assets, and transactions are completed using smart contracts, which ensure that all parties involved in the transaction receive their respective assets and payments.

The Axie Infinity NFT Marketplace has become very popular, with some Axies selling for thousands of dollars. This has led to a new market for digital assets and has given rise to a new wave of blockchain-based games and applications that use NFTs as in-game assets.

9: HOW TO BUY NFTS

I f you're interested in buying NFTs, here's a guide on how to get started.

1. CHOOSE A MARKETPLACE

The first step in buying NFTs is to choose a marketplace. There are many different marketplaces to choose from, each with their own unique features and offerings. A list of popular NFT marketplaces were listed in the previous chapter. It's important to do your research and choose a marketplace that aligns with your interests and goals. A recommendation from a trusted and experienced NFT investor is also very useful.

2. CREATE A WALLET

Before you can buy NFTs, you'll need to create a cryptocurrency wallet that supports the blockchain network used by the marketplace you've chosen. Some popular wallets include MetaMask, Coinbase Wallet, and MyEtherWallet among others. Follow the instructions provided by the wallet provider to create and set up your wallet.

3. FUND YOUR WALLET

Once you've created your wallet, you'll need to fund it with cryptocurrency. Most NFT marketplaces use Ethereum as their preferred cryptocurrency. You can purchase Ethereum on a cryptocurrency exchange like Coinbase, Binance, or Kraken, and then transfer it to your wallet. Be sure to follow the instructions provided by the exchange and the wallet to ensure a successful transfer.

4. BROWSE AND SELECT AN NFT

Now that you have a funded wallet, you can browse the marketplace and select an NFT to purchase. Each marketplace will have its own categories, filters, and search options to help you find NFTs that align with your interests. Once you've found an NFT you're interested in, click on the listing to view more details, such as the artist, the edition number, and the price.

5. MAKE A PURCHASE

If you're ready to buy the NFT, click on the "Buy" or "Bid" button and follow the instructions provided by the marketplace. You may be asked to confirm the transaction and sign it with your wallet's private key. Once the transaction is complete, the NFT will be transferred to your wallet, and you will own the unique digital asset.

6. STORE AND MANAGE YOUR NFT

Now that you own an NFT, it's important to store and manage it properly. Keep your wallet secure and back up your private key to ensure you don't lose access to your NFT. You can view your NFTs in your wallet, and some marketplaces may also offer tools for managing and tracking your NFTs.

7. SELL OR TRADE YOUR NFT

If you decide to sell or trade your NFT, you can do so in the same marketplace where you purchased it or in a different marketplace. Follow the instructions provided by the marketplace to list your NFT for sale or auction. Be aware that there may be fees associated with selling or trading NFTs, and the value of the NFT may fluctuate over time based on market demand.

TIPS FOR BUYING NFTs:

- Do your research and choose a reputable marketplace with a strong track record.
- Understand the value proposition of the NFT before making a purchase. Consider factors such as the artist, the edition number, and the rarity of the asset.

- Keep track of your NFTs and store them securely in your wallet.
- Be prepared for the potential volatility of the NFT market, and don't invest more than you can afford to lose.
- Consider the environmental impact of NFTs, as they require significant amounts of energy to create and trade on blockchain networks.

However, it is important to do your research and understand the risks involved before investing in NFTs. The market is relatively new and volatile, with prices fluctuating rapidly and unpredictably.

If you do decide to invest in NFTs, be sure to only invest what you can afford to lose and consider working with a reputable platform or broker. Look for NFTs with a proven track record of value and consider factors such as the artist's reputation and the rarity of the digital asset.

In addition, it is important to consider the long-term viability of NFTs and their place in the wider art and investment markets. While NFTs have gained a lot of attention in recent years, their future value and importance remain uncertain.

Ultimately, buying NFTs can be a rewarding and exciting experience for those who are willing to do their due diligence and take calculated risks. Whether you are a collector, investor, or simply a fan of digital art, NFTs offer a new and innovative way to own and appreciate digital assets.

10: HOW TO STORE NFTS SECURELY

A s with any valuable asset, it is important to ensure that they are stored securely to protect them from theft or loss.

BEST PRACTICES FOR STORING NFTS SECURELY

1. USE A HARDWARE WALLET

One of the best ways to store NFTs securely is by using a hardware wallet. Hardware wallets are physical devices that store your private keys offline, making it nearly impossible for hackers to access your funds. The two most popular hardware wallets are the Ledger Nano S and the Trezor Model T.

To use a hardware wallet with your NFTs, you will need to connect the device to your computer or smartphone and then transfer your NFTs to the wallet. You can then disconnect the device and store it in a secure location, such as a safe or a safety deposit box.

2. KEEP YOUR PRIVATE KEYS SAFE

Another important aspect of storing NFTs securely is to keep your private keys safe. Private keys are essentially the passwords that allow you to access your NFTs on the blockchain. If your private keys fall into the wrong hands, your NFTs can be stolen or transferred without your permission.

To keep your private keys safe, it is important to use strong passwords and never share them with anyone. You should also consider using a password manager to store your passwords securely and avoid using the same password for multiple accounts.

3. USE A COLD STORAGE WALLET

A cold storage wallet is another type of hardware wallet that is designed to store your NFTs offline. This provides an extra layer of security as your NFTs cannot be accessed by hackers when they are not connected to the internet.

To use a cold storage wallet with your NFTs, you will need to transfer your NFTs to the wallet and then store the device in a secure location. You can then connect the device to the internet when you want to access your NFTs.

4. USE A TRUSTED PLATFORM

If you choose to store your NFTs on a platform, it is important to choose a trusted and reputable platform. Look for platforms that have a track record of security and have implemented strong security measures to protect your NFTs.

When using a platform, it is also important to enable two-factor authentication (2FA) to add an extra layer of security to your account. This will require you to enter a code that is sent to your phone or email before you can access your account.

5. BACK UP YOUR WALLET

Backing up your wallet is an important step in ensuring that your NFTs are secure. If you lose your wallet or it becomes damaged, having a backup will allow you to recover your NFTs.

To back up your wallet, you will need to follow the instructions provided by your wallet provider. This may involve creating a backup phrase or seed that can be used to recover your NFTs in the event of a lost or damaged wallet.

It is important to keep your backup phrase or seed in a safe and secure location, such as a fireproof safe or a safety deposit box. You should also consider creating multiple backups and storing them in different locations to ensure that you always have access to your NFTs.

6. USE STRONG SECURITY MEASURES

In addition to using a hardware wallet and backing up your wallet, it is important to use strong security measures to protect your NFTs. This includes using strong passwords, enabling two-factor authentication, and keeping your computer and software up to date with the latest security updates.

You should also avoid accessing your NFTs on public or unsecured networks, such as public Wi-Fi, as these networks can be easily compromised by hackers.

7. STAY INFORMED

Finally, it is important to stay informed about the latest security threats and best practices for storing NFTs securely. This can be done by following industry news and updates, joining online communities, and attending conferences and events.

By staying informed, you can stay ahead of potential security threats and take proactive measures to protect your NFTs.

***

Storing NFTs securely is an essential aspect of investing in digital assets. By following these best practices, you can ensure that your NFTs are protected from theft, loss, and damage.

While there is no guarantee that your NFTs will never be compromised, taking these steps will greatly reduce the risk of theft or loss. As the world continues to embrace digital assets, it is important to take the necessary precautions to protect your investments and ensure their long-term value.

11: HOW TO SELL NFTS

As the demand for NFTs continues to grow, more and more people are also looking to sell their NFTs for a profit. In this chapter, we will explore the various steps involved in selling NFTs and provide some tips on how to maximize your returns.

1. DETERMINE THE VALUE OF YOUR NFT

The first step in selling an NFT is to determine its value. This can be a complex process as the value of NFTs can vary greatly depending on a variety of factors, including the rarity of the item, the quality of the artwork or design, the popularity of the artist or creator, and the current market demand.

One way to determine the value of your NFT is to research similar items that have been sold in the past. This can give you a general idea of the price range that your NFT may fall into. There are also online marketplaces and auction sites that can provide you with more specific pricing information for NFTs.

2. CHOOSE A PLATFORM TO SELL YOUR NFT

Once you have determined the value of your NFT, the next step is to choose a platform to sell it on. There are a variety of platforms available for selling NFTs, each with their own unique features and requirements.

Some of the most popular NFT marketplaces include OpenSea, Nifty Gateway, SuperRare, and Rarible. These platforms offer a range of services, including the ability to create and list your NFT for sale, connect with buyers, and receive payment.

Before choosing a platform, it is important to research and compare the fees, policies, and user experiences of each one to determine which one is the best fit for your needs.

3. LIST YOUR NFT FOR SALE

Once you have chosen a platform, the next step is to list your NFT for sale. This involves creating a listing that includes a description of your NFT, images or videos of the item, and the asking price.

It is important to provide as much detail as possible about your NFT, including any relevant information about the artist or creator, the history of the item, and any notable features that make it unique.

When setting the asking price for your NFT, it is important to consider the current market demand, the value of similar items that have been sold in the past, and any fees or commissions that may be charged by the platform.

4. PROMOTE YOUR NFT

Once your NFT is listed for sale, the next step is to promote it to potential buyers. This can be done in a variety of ways, including social media marketing, email marketing, and paid advertising.

Social media platforms like Twitter, Instagram, and TikTok can be powerful tools for promoting your NFT to a large audience. You can also reach out to influencers and media outlets to help spread the word about your item.

Email marketing can be an effective way to reach out to potential buyers who have expressed interest in NFTs or have previously purchased similar items. Paid advertising can also be an option, although this can be more costly and may require a larger budget.

5. CLOSE THE SALE

Once you have found a buyer for your NFT, the next step is to close the sale. This involves transferring ownership of the NFT to the buyer and receiving payment for the item.

Most NFT marketplaces have built-in tools for transferring ownership of NFTs and processing payments. These tools typically involve using a smart contract to verify the transaction and ensure that both parties receive what they are owed.

Before completing the sale, it is important to ensure that the NFT being sold is authentic and legitimate. This can involve verifying the provenance of the NFT, ensuring that it was created by the claimed artist or creator, and confirming that it is not a duplicate or a fake. In addition, buyers should be aware of any potential copyright or intellectual property issues related to the NFT they are purchasing.

Once the authenticity of the NFT has been established, the transaction can proceed. The buyer typically sends the payment in cryptocurrency to the seller, and the smart contract verifies the transaction and transfers ownership of the NFT to the buyer. The transaction is recorded on the blockchain, which serves as a permanent and transparent ledger of all NFT transactions.

One of the benefits of NFTs is that they can be easily traded or sold on secondary markets, providing opportunities for investors and collectors to buy and sell NFTs for a profit. However, it is important to keep in mind that the value of NFTs can be highly volatile, and prices can fluctuate rapidly based on market demand and other factors.

As with any investment or purchase, it is important to do your research and understand the risks involved before buying or selling NFTs. It is also important to use reputable NFT marketplaces and to be cautious of scams or fraudulent activity in the NFT space.

12: NFT VALUATION AND PRICING

Having a good understanding of how NFT value is determined and how prices are set is useful to every NFT investor.

VALUING NFTs

Valuing NFTs is a complex process that involves considering a variety of factors, including the rarity, provenance, and demand for the item being sold. In many ways, the valuation of NFTs is similar to the valuation of traditional collectibles like rare stamps or coins.

One of the key factors that can influence the value of an NFT is its rarity. Items that are one-of-a-kind or part of a limited series are often highly sought after and can command high prices. For example, the first tweet ever sent by Twitter founder Jack Dorsey was sold as an NFT for $2.9 million in March 2021. The fact that this tweet is a unique item that cannot be replicated or duplicated is a major factor in its high valuation.

Another important factor in valuing NFTs is their provenance. This refers to the history and authenticity of the item being sold. For example, an NFT created by a well-known artist or musician may be more valuable than an NFT created by an unknown or emerging artist. Similarly, NFTs that can be traced back to their original creators and have a clear chain of ownership may be more highly valued than NFTs with uncertain origins.

Demand is also a key factor in valuing NFTs. Items that are highly sought after by collectors or investors may command higher prices than similar items with less demand. This can be influenced by a variety of factors, including the popularity of the artist or creator, current market trends, and the perceived cultural or historical significance of the item being sold.

SETTING NFT PRICES

Once the value of an NFT has been determined, the next step is to set a price for the item. This can be a challenging process, as there is often a great deal of uncertainty and volatility in the NFT market. Prices can fluctuate rapidly based on a variety of factors, and it can be difficult to predict how demand will evolve over time.

One approach to setting NFT prices is to use a traditional auction model. This involves setting a starting price and allowing buyers to bid on the item until a final price is reached. Auctions can be an effective way to determine the market value of an NFT, as they allow buyers to compete with one another and drive up the price.

Another approach to setting NFT prices is to use a fixed price model. This involves setting a price for the item based on its estimated value and allowing buyers to purchase it at that price. Fixed price models can be more predictable and stable than auction models, but they may not capture the full market value of an NFT if demand is higher than expected.

Some NFT marketplaces are experimenting with dynamic pricing models that use algorithms to adjust prices in real time based on market demand. This approach is still in its early stages, but it has the potential to provide a more flexible and responsive pricing mechanism for NFTs.

FACTORS AFFECTING NFT PRICES

There are a variety of factors that can affect the price of NFTs. Some of the most important include:

Rarity

Items that are one-of-a-kind or part of a limited series are often highly sought after and can command high prices.

Provenance

NFTs that can be traced back to their original creators and have a clear chain of ownership may be more highly valued than NFTs with uncertain origins. This is because provenance adds to the authenticity and history of an NFT, making it more valuable to collectors and investors.

Popularity of the creator

NFTs created by well-known artists or musicians may be more valuable than NFTs created by unknown or emerging creators. This is because the reputation and popularity of the creator can influence demand for the item.

Cultural and historical significance

NFTs that have cultural or historical significance may be more valuable than similar items without such significance. For example, an NFT that is associated with a significant cultural moment or movement may be more valuable than a similar NFT that is not.

Market trends

The NFT market is subject to trends and fads, which can influence demand and prices. For example, there may be a sudden surge in demand for NFTs related to a particular video game or meme, which can drive up prices for those items.

Scarcity of the underlying asset

NFTs that are associated with scarce or valuable underlying assets may be more valuable than similar NFTs associated with more common or less valuable assets. For example, an NFT that represents ownership of a rare virtual real estate property may be more valuable than an NFT representing ownership of a more common virtual item.

NAVIGATING THE NFT MARKET

As with any investment or purchase, it bears repeating the important to approach NFTs with caution and do your research before buying or selling. The NFT market is still relatively new and rapidly evolving, which means that prices and trends can be unpredictable.

One key factor to keep in mind is the potential for volatility in NFT prices. While some NFTs have sold for millions of dollars, prices can also drop rapidly if market demand shifts or if a particular trend or fad loses popularity. It is important to approach NFTs as a long-term investment and to carefully consider the risks and potential rewards before making a purchase.

It is also important to use reputable NFT marketplaces and to be cautious of scams and fraudulent activity in the NFT space. There have been reports of fake NFTs being sold on unregulated marketplaces, as well as instances of fraudulent sellers taking advantage of buyers. It is important to thoroughly research the seller and the item being sold before making a purchase, and to use reputable platforms that offer buyer protections and dispute resolution mechanisms.

In addition, it can be helpful to seek out expert guidance when navigating the NFT market. This can include consulting with NFT collectors and investors, as well as industry experts who can provide insights into market trends and pricing models.

Ultimately, the future of NFTs will depend on a variety of factors, including the continued growth and evolution of the underlying technology, the development of new use cases and applications, and the ongoing interest and demand from collectors and investors. While there are still many questions and uncertainties surrounding the future of NFTs, they have already proven to be a powerful and exciting tool for creators, collectors, and investors alike.

13: NFT INVESTING STRATEGIES

In this chapter, we will explore some NFT investing strategies that you can use to make informed decisions and maximize your returns.

NFT INVESTING STRATEGIES

Do Your Research

As with any investment, it's important to do your research before buying an NFT. Research the artist or creator behind the NFT, the history of the piece, and any other relevant information that can help you determine its value. Look for NFTs that are rare or have a unique story behind them, as these are likely to appreciate in value over time.

Consider the Long-Term Potential

When investing in NFTs, it's important to consider the long-term potential of the asset. Look for NFTs that are likely to hold their value over time, such as those created by well-known artists or those with historical significance. Avoid investing in NFTs solely based on short-term hype or trends, as these assets may not hold their value in the long run.

Diversify Your Portfolio

Just like with traditional investments, it's important to diversify your NFT portfolio. Invest in a range of NFTs across different categories, such as art, music, and collectibles. This can help reduce your risk and ensure that your portfolio is well-rounded.

Understand the Market

NFTs are a new and evolving market, so it's important to keep up with the latest trends and developments. Follow NFT news and developments closely, and be prepared to adapt your investment strategy as the market evolves.

Set a Budget

As with any investment, it's important to set a budget for your NFT investments. Determine how much you are willing to invest and stick to that budget. Avoid investing more than you can afford to lose, as the NFT market can be volatile and unpredictable.

Consider the Platform

When buying NFTs, you'll need to choose a platform to purchase them from. It's important to research the platform before making any purchases, as some platforms may be more reputable than others. Look for platforms with a strong track record of sales and positive reviews from buyers and sellers.

Understand the Fees

When buying and selling NFTs, you'll need to pay fees to the platform and the blockchain network. These fees can vary depending on the platform and the size of the transaction. Make sure you understand the fees associated with buying and selling NFTs before making any transactions, as they can eat into your profits. As a first timer, you may not have a good handle on the fees, but as you gain experience and knowledge, you will be in a better position to evaluate marketplaces and chose one that works better for you.

Consider the Storage

NFTs are stored on a blockchain, but you'll also need to consider how you'll store the digital asset itself. Some platforms offer built-in storage solutions, while others may require you to store the NFT in a digital wallet. Make sure you understand the storage options available to you and choose a solution that is secure and reliable.

Seek Professional Advice

If you're new to NFT investing or are unsure about your investment strategy, it's a good idea to seek professional advice. Consider consulting with a financial advisor or investment professional who has experience in the NFT market. They can provide you with guidance and help you make informed decisions about your investments.

Stay Up To Date

Finally, it's important to stay up to date with the latest developments in the NFT market. Follow industry news and trends closely, and be prepared to adapt your investment strategy as the market evolves. Attend conferences and events to network with other NFT investors and stay informed about the latest developments in the industry.

14: RISKS AND CHALLENGES OF NFT INVESTING

E very investment carries a level of risk. The higher the risk, the higher the reward. The risk in every investment lies mostly in the fact that investor does not know what they are doing. The more knowledgeable and skillful you are, the better you can handle or minimize the risks.

RISKS OF NFT INVESTING

Let's explore some of the potential risks of NFT investing.

1. Market Volatility

Like any emerging market, the NFT market is highly volatile. Prices can fluctuate rapidly, and it's not uncommon to see NFTs selling for millions of dollars one day and then plummeting in value the next. This volatility can make it difficult to predict future trends and make informed investment decisions.

2. Lack of Liquidity

Another challenge with NFT investing is the lack of liquidity. Unlike traditional assets like stocks or bonds, NFTs can be difficult to sell quickly. There may not be a buyer available when you're ready to sell, or the buyer may not be willing to pay the price you're asking. This lack of liquidity can make it challenging to exit an investment when you need to.

3. Lack of Regulation

The NFT market is largely unregulated, which means that there's a greater risk of fraud and scams. There have already been several high-profile cases of NFT scams, where buyers have paid large sums of money for an NFT only to find out that it wasn't authentic. This lack of regulation makes it important to do your due diligence and only invest in NFTs that you're confident are legitimate.

4. Technical Challenges

Investing in NFTs requires a certain level of technical expertise. You need to be familiar with blockchain technology, digital wallets, and other technical concepts in order to participate in the NFT market. This can be a barrier for some investors, and it's important to be prepared to invest the time and effort to learn about these concepts before you start investing.

5. Sustainability Concerns

Another potential risk of NFT investing is the environmental impact. The process of creating and selling NFTs requires a significant amount of energy, which has led to concerns about the environmental impact of this new market. Some critics have even gone so far as to label NFTs as a "carbon bomb" due to their high energy consumption.

TIPS FOR MINIMIZING RISKS

Despite these risks, there are steps you can take to minimize your risk when investing in NFTs. Here are a few tips to keep in mind:

1. Do Your Research

Before investing in any NFT, it's important to do your research. This means understanding what an NFT is, how it works, and what the potential risks and benefits are. You should also research the specific NFT you are considering buying, including its history, creator, and any associated contracts or terms.

2. Understand the Market

Like any investment, the NFT market is subject to fluctuations and trends. It's important to stay up-to-date on the latest news and developments in the market, as well as to understand the factors that may affect the value of your NFT. This includes factors like the popularity of the creator, the rarity of the NFT, and the overall demand for digital assets.

3. Consider the Long-Term

While it can be tempting to buy and sell NFTs quickly in an effort to make a quick profit, it's important to consider the long-term potential of your investment. This means thinking about how the NFT may appreciate in value over time, as well as considering any potential risks or downsides to holding onto it.

4. Be Prepared For Volatility

Like any investment, the value of an NFT can be subject to volatility and fluctuation. This means that you should be prepared for the possibility of your investment losing value, as well as the possibility of it increasing in value. It's important to have a solid understanding of the risks and potential rewards before investing in an NFT.

5. Choose a Reputable Platform

When buying and selling NFTs, it's important to choose a reputable platform or marketplace. Look for a platform that has a strong reputation, good user reviews, and a solid track record of facilitating secure and reliable transactions. You should also consider the fees and commissions associated with the platform, as well as any potential risks or limitations.

6. Stay Informed and Connected

Finally, it's important to stay informed and connected in the NFT community. This means following the latest news and trends, as well as connecting with other NFT investors and enthusiasts. This can help you stay up-to-date on the latest opportunities and developments, as well as provide you with valuable insights and advice.

15: LEGAL AND REGULATORY ISSUES SURROUNDING NFTS

One of the biggest legal issues surrounding NFTs is copyright infringement. While the blockchain technology that underpins NFTs makes them difficult to duplicate, it is still possible for someone to create an NFT that infringes on someone else's copyright.

For example, if an artist creates a piece of artwork and someone else creates an NFT of that artwork without permission. That would be an obvious violation of the artist's copyright.

This issue is further complicated by the fact that many NFT marketplaces do not have clear policies in place for dealing with copyright infringement, leaving creators vulnerable to having their work stolen or misused.

Another legal issue that arises with NFTs is taxation. In the United States, NFTs are generally treated as property for tax purposes, which means that any profits made from the sale of an NFT are subject to capital gains tax.

However, the rules around NFT taxation are still somewhat murky, and it is unclear how exactly the IRS will enforce these rules. This creates a level of uncertainty for buyers and sellers of NFTs, as they may not be sure exactly how much they will owe in taxes when they sell an NFT.

Regulatory issues are also a concern when it comes to NFTs. Because NFTs are a relatively new technology, there is not yet a clear regulatory framework in place for them. This means that there is potential for fraud and other illegal activities to take place within the NFT market, as there are few regulations in place to prevent it.

For example, it is possible for someone to create an NFT that claims to represent ownership of a piece of artwork or other content, even if they do not actually have the rights to that content. This could lead to unsuspecting buyers spending large sums of money on NFTs that are essentially worthless.

Another potential regulatory issue with NFTs is their impact on the environment. The process of creating and selling NFTs requires a significant amount of energy, which can have a negative impact on the environment.

Additionally, many of the marketplaces where NFTs are sold have policies in place that encourage high-volume trading, which can lead to even more energy consumption. This issue has led to criticism of NFTs from some environmental activists, who argue that the technology is contributing to climate change.

Finally, there are issues surrounding the sale and transfer of NFTs. Because NFTs are a digital asset, it can be difficult to prove ownership or transfer ownership from one party to another.

While blockchain technology provides some level of security and transparency, it is still possible for someone to sell an NFT that they do not actually own, or for ownership of an NFT to become unclear over time. This can lead to disputes over ownership and potentially even legal action.

In order to address these legal and regulatory issues surrounding NFTs, there are several steps that can be taken.

Firstly, it is important for NFT marketplaces to have clear policies in place for dealing with copyright infringement. This could include measures such as requiring sellers to provide proof of ownership or licensing agreements for any content being sold as an NFT. Additionally, marketplaces could implement systems for reporting and removing infringing content, and work with copyright holders to resolve any disputes that arise.

Secondly, governments could take steps to clarify the taxation rules surrounding NFTs. This could include providing clear guidance on how capital gains tax should be calculated for NFT sales, as well as implementing regulations to prevent tax evasion and fraud within the NFT market.

Thirdly, there is a need for greater regulatory oversight of NFTs to prevent fraudulent activity and ensure that marketplaces are operating in a fair and transparent manner. This could include measures such as requiring marketplaces to register with regulatory bodies and comply with certain standards and best practices.

Fourthly, there is a need to address the environmental impact of NFTs. This could include exploring ways to reduce the energy consumption required to create and trade NFTs, as well as encouraging marketplaces to adopt more sustainable practices.

Finally, there is a need for greater transparency and accountability when it comes to the sale and transfer of NFTs. This could include measures such as implementing a system for tracking ownership of NFTs on the blockchain, and providing clear guidelines for how ownership disputes should be resolved.

16: TAX IMPLICATIONS
OF NFT INVESTING

s with any investment, including NFTs, it is important to consider the tax implications of investing in them.

CAPITAL GAINS TAX

One of the most important tax implications to consider when investing in NFTs is capital gains tax. When an NFT is sold for more than it was originally purchased for, the difference is considered a capital gain. Capital gains tax is the tax that is paid on the profit from the sale of an asset. The rate at which capital gains tax is applied depends on the holding period of the asset and the investor's tax bracket.

SHORT-TERM CAPITAL GAINS

Short-term capital gains are applied to assets that are held for less than a year before being sold. These gains are taxed at the investor's ordinary income tax rate, which can range from 10% to 37%. If an investor purchases an NFT and sells it within a year for a profit, they will be subject to short-term capital gains tax.

LONG-TERM CAPITAL GAINS

Long-term capital gains are applied to assets that are held for more than a year before being sold. These gains are taxed at a lower rate than short-term gains and depend on the investor's tax bracket. The tax rate for long-term capital gains ranges from 0% to 20%.

For example, if an investor purchases an NFT for $1,000 and sells it for $5,000 after holding it for 14 months, they would be subject to long-term capital gains tax. If their tax bracket is 15%, they would owe $600 in capital gains tax ($4,000 gain x 15% tax rate).

LIKE-KIND EXCHANGES

Another tax implication to consider when investing in NFTs is the ability to use like-kind exchanges. Like-kind exchanges allow investors to defer paying capital gains tax by exchanging one asset for another similar asset. For example, if an investor sells one NFT for a profit and then immediately purchases another NFT, they may be able to defer paying capital gains tax on the first NFT by using the like-kind exchange rule.

However, it is important to note that the like-kind exchange rule only applies to assets that are used for business or investment purposes. Therefore, it is unclear whether NFTs can be considered a like-kind asset. The IRS has not yet issued guidance on this matter, so investors should consult with a tax professional before using the like-kind exchange rule for NFTs.

DEDUCTING LOSSES

While investors hope to make a profit when investing in NFTs, it is important to consider the possibility of losses. If an investor sells an NFT for less than they purchased it for, the difference is considered a capital loss. Capital losses can be used to offset capital gains, reducing the amount of capital gains tax owed. If the total amount of capital losses is greater than the amount of capital gains, up to $3,000 in capital losses can be deducted from the investor's taxable income in a given tax year. Any remaining capital losses can be carried forward to future tax years.

It is important to keep accurate records of NFT purchases and sales to accurately calculate capital gains or losses. Investors should document the date of purchase, purchase price, date of sale, and sale price for each NFT transaction. This information can be used to calculate the holding period and gain or loss for each transaction.

SELF-EMPLOYMENT TAX

For individuals who create and sell their own NFTs, self-employment tax may also apply. Self-employment tax is a tax on income earned from self-employment activities. If an individual creates and sells their own NFTs as a business, they may be subject to self-employment tax on the profits from those sales.

The self-employment tax rate is currently 15.3% and applies to the first $142,800 of net self-employment income. Any additional self-employment income is subject to a 2.9% Medicare tax.

NFTs AS INVESTMENTS

Investing in NFTs can be seen as a speculative investment, much like investing in stocks or cryptocurrencies. While NFTs can be a unique investment opportunity, they come with their own set of risks and uncertainties. Like any investment, investors should carefully consider the potential risks and rewards of investing in NFTs.

In addition to tax implications, investors should also consider the potential for NFTs to lose value over time. NFTs are a new and rapidly evolving market, and there is no guarantee that their value will continue to rise. It is important to approach NFT investing with caution and to only invest what you can afford to lose.

Investing in NFTs can be a unique and exciting investment opportunity. However, it is important to consider the tax implications of investing in NFTs. Capital gains tax, like-kind exchanges, deducting losses, and self-employment tax are all important factors to consider when investing in NFTs.

Investors should keep accurate records of NFT purchases and sales to accurately calculate capital gains or losses. They should also consult with a tax professional to ensure that they are following all applicable tax laws and regulations.

As with any investment, it is important to do your own

research and make informed decisions. By carefully considering the tax implications and potential risks and rewards of NFT investing, investors can make informed decisions that align with their financial goals and objectives.

17: FAMOUS NFT SALES AND THEIR IMPACT ON THE MARKET

Several high-profile NFT sales made headlines, including the $69 million sale of Beeple's "Everydays: The First 5000 Days" at Christie's auction house in March 2021.

Here are some other famous NFT sales and their impact on the market:

"CRYPTOPUNK #3100" - $69 MILLION

In May 2021, a single CryptoPunk NFT was sold for a record-breaking $69 million at a Christie's auction. The CryptoPunk #3100, which features a punk with a mohawk and green goggles, was sold to an anonymous buyer and quickly became the most expensive NFT ever sold.

The sale of CryptoPunk #3100 had a significant impact on the NFT market, as it demonstrated the incredible value that collectors were willing to pay for these digital assets. It also helped to cement CryptoPunks as one of the most popular and valuable NFT collections.

"THE FIRST 5000 DAYS" - $69 MILLION

Beeple's "Everydays: The First 5000 Days" NFT sale at Christie's in March 2021 was another major milestone for the NFT market. The digital artwork, which features a collage of Beeple's daily drawings from 2007 to 2021, was sold for a staggering $69 million to an NFT fund called Metapurse.

The sale of "The First 5000 Days" helped to put NFTs on the

map, as it was one of the first high-profile NFT sales to receive widespread media attention. It also demonstrated the value of NFTs as a new asset class and paved the way for more artists and collectors to get involved in the NFT market.

"CRYPTOKITTIES" - $170,000

CryptoKitties, a collection of digital cats that can be bought, sold, and bred, was one of the first NFT collections to gain popularity. In December 2017, a single CryptoKitty sold for a then-record-breaking 246 ETH, which was worth approximately $117,000 at the time.

The sale of CryptoKitties had a significant impact on the NFT market, as it demonstrated the potential value of NFT collections and helped to spark interest in the emerging asset class.

"THE FUNGIBLE COLLECTION" - $2.2 MILLION

In June 2021, artist Trevor Jones sold "The Fungible Collection," a set of 101 NFTs that represent a single painting, for $2.2 million. The collection included one unique NFT and 100 fungible tokens, which could be traded and sold separately.

The sale of "The Fungible Collection" demonstrated the versatility of NFTs, as it showed that they could be used to represent both unique and divisible assets. It also helped to solidify Trevor Jones' position as one of the most popular and innovative NFT artists.

"FOREVER ROSE" - $1 MILLION

In February 2018, artist Kevin Abosch sold a digital artwork called "Forever Rose" for $1 million. The artwork is a digital representation of a rose that never fades and is intended to symbolize eternal love.

The sale of "Forever Rose" was significant because it demonstrated the potential of NFTs to represent intangible concepts like love and emotion. It also showed that NFTs could be used to create unique and valuable digital artworks that could be owned and traded like traditional physical art.

"RIGHT-CLICK AND SAVE AS GUY" - $7 MILLION

London-based artist XCopy employs a deconstructed aesthetic that bears resemblance to the paintings of Basquiat, but in a digital format. In XCopy's art pieces, various types of image distortions and noises, similar to those caused by computer glitches or malfunctions, are intentionally integrated.

These unique digital creations, referred to as NFTs, are highly coveted and often fetch several million dollars. Just last month, one of XCopy's NFTs was sold for 1,600 ether (equivalent to $7.09 million) via SuperRare, and was purchased by none other than Snoop Dogg's NFT pseudonym, "Cozomo de Medici".

***

These high-profile NFT sales have had a significant impact on the NFT market. They have helped to legitimize NFTs as a new asset class, attracting more artists, collectors, and investors to the market. They have also demonstrated the incredible value that collectors are willing to pay for these digital assets, paving the way for more high-priced NFT sales in the future.

One of the key drivers of the NFT market is the scarcity of these digital assets. Unlike physical art, which can be replicated or reproduced, NFTs are unique and verifiable, making them highly sought after by collectors. This scarcity has driven up the value of NFTs, with some collectors willing to pay millions of dollars for a single digital asset.

Another factor driving the NFT market is the growing interest in cryptocurrency and blockchain technology. NFTs are recorded on a blockchain, making them secure, transparent, and verifiable.

This technology has the potential to revolutionize the art world, creating a new ecosystem for artists, collectors, and investors to buy and sell digital art.

As the NFT market continues to grow and evolve, it will be interesting to see how it transforms the art world and what impact it has on the broader cryptocurrency and blockchain ecosystem. With high-profile sales like Beeple's "Everydays: The First 5000 Days" and the record-breaking sale of CryptoPunk #3100, it is clear that NFTs are not just a passing trend but a significant new asset class that is here to stay.

18: FUTURE OF NFTS AND THEIR POTENTIAL IMPACT ON THE ART WORLD

While the rise of NFTs has been met with skepticism from some in the art world, many experts believe that they have the potential to transform the way that art is bought, sold, and displayed.

One of the key benefits of NFTs is that they allow artists to monetize digital art in a way that was previously impossible.

Before NFTs, digital artworks could be easily copied and distributed, making it difficult for artists to control the distribution and monetization of their work.

With NFTs, artists can create unique, verifiable, and valuable digital artworks that can be sold and traded like traditional physical art. This has the potential to create new revenue streams for artists, allowing them to earn a living from their digital creations.

Another potential benefit of NFTs is that they could democratize the art world, making it more accessible to a wider range of artists and collectors.

Traditionally, the art world has been dominated by a small number of wealthy collectors and institutions, making it difficult for emerging artists to gain exposure and recognition. With NFTs, however, artists can reach a global audience of collectors and buyers, regardless of their location or status in the traditional art world. This has the potential to level the playing field for emerging artists, giving them a platform to showcase their work and build their careers.

In addition to these benefits, NFTs also have the potential to transform the way that art is displayed and experienced. With NFTs, artists can create digital artworks that are interactive, immersive, and dynamic.

These artworks can be displayed in virtual galleries, museums, and other digital spaces, allowing viewers to experience them in a way that is not possible with traditional physical art. This has the potential to create new forms of artistic expression and to redefine what it means to experience art.

Despite the many potential benefits of NFTs, there are also concerns about their long-term viability and sustainability. One major concern is the environmental impact of NFTs. Another concern is the speculative nature of NFTs, which has led some to question their long-term value and stability as an asset class.

Despite these concerns, the NFT market is showing no signs of slowing down. In fact, it is evolving and expanding, with new types of NFTs emerging all the time.

One example is social media NFTs, which allow users to monetize their social media posts and followers. Another example is virtual real estate NFTs, which allow buyers to purchase and own virtual plots of land in virtual worlds like Decentraland.

As the NFT market continues to grow and evolve, it will be interesting to see how it transforms the art world and what impact it has on the broader cryptocurrency and blockchain ecosystem.

Some experts believe that NFTs could revolutionize the art world, creating a new ecosystem for artists, collectors, and investors to buy and sell digital art. Others are more skeptical, arguing that NFTs are a passing fad or a speculative bubble that is bound to burst.

Despite these differing opinions, one thing is clear: NFTs have already had a significant impact on the art world and are poised to continue to do so in the future.

As more and more artists create and sell NFTs, and more collectors and investors buy and trade them, the market is likely to become more sophisticated and nuanced. This could lead to the development of new business models, such as fractional ownership, where multiple investors own a share of a single NFT, or NFT exchanges, where NFTs can be traded like traditional securities.

In addition to these developments, NFTs are also likely to play a role in the broader trend towards digitalization and decentralization. With more and more aspects of our lives moving online, from work to socializing, it seems likely that the art world will follow suit. NFTs have the potential to create a new paradigm for art ownership, one that is not tied to physical space or location.

This could lead to a more global and interconnected art world, where artists from around the world can connect with collectors and buyers from different countries and cultures. It could also lead to a more diverse and inclusive art world, where artists from underrepresented communities have a platform to share their work and be recognized for their contributions.

Of course, there are still many challenges that need to be addressed if NFTs are to reach their full potential. These include issues around sustainability, security, and regulation. It is important that the NFT market is developed in a responsible and sustainable way, one that takes into account the environmental impact of blockchain technology and the need for secure and transparent transactions.

There is also a need for greater regulation and oversight of the NFT market, to ensure that it is not used for illegal activities such as money laundering or fraud. Some countries, such as China, have already taken steps to regulate the NFT market, and it seems likely that others will follow suit in the coming years.

Despite these challenges, the future of NFTs in the art world looks bright. With their ability to create unique and verifiable digital assets, NFTs have the potential to revolutionize the way that art is bought, sold, and experienced. They have already created new opportunities for artists, collectors, and investors, and are likely to continue to do so in the years to come.

As the NFT market continues to evolve, it will be important for all stakeholders to work together to ensure that it is developed in a responsible and sustainable way. This will require collaboration between artists, collectors, investors, regulators, and other stakeholders, to create a market that is both innovative and inclusive.

19: COMMON NFT SCAMS AND HOW TO AVOID THEM

With the NFT boom, it is no surprise to have scammers on the prowl looking for unsuspecting investors to defraud. Below are some common NFT scams you should be aware of:

1. FAKE NFTs

Scammers may create fake NFTs that mimic popular and valuable NFTs. These fake NFTs may look like the real thing, but they do not have any value or authenticity.

2. PHISHING SCAMS

Scammers may create fake NFT platforms or social media accounts and ask users to share their private keys or wallet information. This information can be used to steal NFTs or other cryptocurrencies.

3. NFT GIVEAWAYS

This works as a phishing scam with a slight variation. Also referred to as airdrop scams, fraudsters lure victims into promoting an NFT and registering on their website with the promise of receiving a complimentary NFT. However, upon completion, the scammers will provide a link that prompts the victim to input their wallet information to claim the reward. By doing so, the scammers gain access to the victim's account details and can pilfer their NFT collection.

4. PUMP-AND-DUMP SCHEMES

Scammers may artificially inflate the price of a new NFT project by purchasing large amounts of tokens and then selling them for a profit. This can cause the value of the NFT to crash and leave buyers with worthless tokens.

5. BIDDING SCAMS

Bidding scams are prevalent in the secondary market, especially when selling your NFT. As you list your NFT for sale, scammers may place the highest bid, which could prompt you to sell it to them. However, these fraudsters may alter the cryptocurrency used for the bidding (to a much cheaper crypto) without your awareness.

6. PONZI SCHEMES

Scammers may promise high returns on NFT investments, but instead use new investors' money to pay off earlier investors. This type of scheme is unsustainable and will eventually collapse, leaving investors with significant losses.

7. INVESTOR SCAMS

Involves the creation of seemingly legitimate NFT projects that are falsely promoted as profitable investments. These projects, however, hold no value in reality. Once the fraudsters accumulate enough funds from investors, they disappear without leaving any trace.

Here are some tips for avoiding NFT scams:

Do Your Research

Before buying an NFT, research the seller and the platform on which the NFT is being sold. Look for reviews and feedback from other buyers to ensure that the seller is reputable.

Verify Authenticity

Verify that the NFT is authentic and not a copy by checking the blockchain for proof of ownership and verifying that the seller is the true owner of the NFT.

Beware of Phishing Scams

Be wary of unsolicited emails or messages claiming to be from an NFT platform or seller. These could be phishing scams designed to steal your personal information or NFTs. Contact the marketplace directly using known contacts rather than responding to or clicking strange links.

Check the Contract Terms

Make sure to read and understand the contract terms before buying an NFT. Some contracts may include hidden fees or restrictions on the use of the NFT. If you are selling, always double-check which crypto you're being paid with and be sure not to accept anything less than the agreed-upon bidding offer.

Use a Trusted Platform

Only buy NFTs from trusted platforms that have a track record of secure transactions and customer support.

Verify the Project and Team

Check the background and history of the project and team behind the NFT. Verify that they have a legitimate and credible reputation within the industry.

Trust Your Instincts

If something seems too good to be true, it probably is. Use your common sense and trust your instincts when buying NFTs. If you have any doubts, it's better to err on the side of caution and not make the purchase.

20: IS NFT INVESTING RIGHT FOR YOU?

W hile NFTs may offer new opportunities for creators and collectors, they may not be right for everyone. Here are some key factors to consider before investing in NFTs.

RISK TOLERANCE

As with any type of investment, investing in NFTs comes with a certain degree of risk. The value of NFTs can be highly volatile, and there is no guarantee that you will be able to sell your NFT for a profit. It is important to consider your risk tolerance before investing in NFTs and to only invest money that you can afford to lose.

KNOWLEDGE AND EXPERIENCE

Investing in NFTs requires a certain level of knowledge and experience. You will need to understand how blockchain technology works, how to navigate digital marketplaces, and how to evaluate the potential value of a particular NFT. If you are new to the world of cryptocurrencies and blockchain technology, it may be wise to start with a small investment and do your research before investing more.

INVESTMENT GOALS

It is important to consider your investment goals before investing in NFTs. Are you looking to make a quick profit, or are you investing for the long-term? Do you have other income sources, or you are betting the house on NFTs? Do you have a specific NFT in mind, or are you open to exploring different opportunities? Knowing your investment goals can help you make more informed decisions about which NFTs to invest in and when to buy and sell.

TAX IMPLICATIONS

Investing in NFTs can have tax implications, and it is important to understand these implications before investing. In the United States, for example, NFTs are generally treated as property for tax purposes, which means that you may need to pay capital gains taxes when you sell your NFT for a profit. It is important to consult with a tax professional before investing in NFTs to ensure that you understand your tax obligations.

TECHNICAL CHALLENGES

Investing in NFTs can also come with technical challenges. For example, you may need to set up a digital wallet to store your NFTs, or you may need to navigate unfamiliar marketplaces and trading platforms. If you are not comfortable with technology or if you do not have experience with cryptocurrencies, investing in NFTs may be more challenging for you.

Investing in NFTs can be a lucrative opportunity for those who are willing to take on the risks and challenges that come with it. However, it is important to consider your risk tolerance, investment goals, knowledge and experience, tax implications, and technical abilities before diving into the world of NFT investing. With careful research and thoughtful consideration, you can make informed decisions that help you navigate this emerging market.

It is important to remember that NFTs are a relatively new technology and the market is still developing. As with any investment, it is crucial to do your due diligence and research potential investments thoroughly. This includes evaluating the authenticity and uniqueness of an NFT, assessing the demand for the asset, and considering any potential legal or regulatory issues.

One of the key benefits of NFTs is that they can provide a more direct connection between creators and collectors. By cutting out intermediaries such as galleries or auction houses, NFTs can offer artists and collectors more control over the buying and selling process. However, this also means that the market can be highly competitive, with many other investors vying for the same assets.

It is important to keep in mind that the value of NFTs can be highly volatile. While some NFTs have sold for millions of dollars, others may not retain their value over time. It is important to have a clear investment strategy and to be prepared for the possibility that your NFT may not appreciate in value as quickly or as significantly as you had hoped.

Another consideration is the technical aspect of investing in NFTs. This includes setting up a digital wallet to store your NFTs, understanding the mechanics of blockchain technology, and navigating digital marketplaces and trading platforms. It is important to have a basic understanding of these technical aspects before investing in NFTs.

Finally, it is important to consider the tax implications of investing in NFTs. In the United States, for example, NFTs are generally treated as property for tax purposes. This means that if you sell an NFT for a profit, you may need to pay capital gains taxes on that profit. It is important to consult with a tax professional to understand your tax obligations before investing in NFTs.

***

NFTs can offer a unique investment opportunity for those who are willing to take on the risks and challenges that come with this emerging market. However, it is important to carefully evaluate your risk tolerance, investment goals, knowledge and experience, tax obligations, and technical abilities before investing in NFTs. With careful consideration and research, you can make informed decisions that help you navigate this exciting and dynamic market.

21: CONCLUSION AND NEXT STEPS

Congratulations! You have reached the end of **NFT Investing 101: A Beginner's Guide to Collectible Digital Assets.** Throughout this book, we have explored the exciting world of non-fungible tokens (NFTs) and how they have revolutionized the concept of digital ownership. You have learned about the basics of NFTs, the different types of NFT marketplaces, the potential risks and rewards of investing in NFTs, and strategies to make informed investment decisions.

As you now understand, NFTs have emerged as a vibrant and dynamic asset class, offering unique opportunities for both creators and investors. These digital assets have gained significant traction across various industries, including art, gaming, sports, and entertainment. NFTs allow creators to monetize their digital works and provide collectors with a new way to own and trade digital assets.

In this concluding chapter, we will summarize the key takeaways from this book and provide some suggestions for further education and learning in the realm of NFT investing.

KEY TAKEAWAYS:

1. NFTs are unique digital assets that represent ownership or proof of authenticity for a particular item, whether it's artwork, music, collectibles, virtual real estate, or more.

2. NFTs are powered by blockchain technology, providing transparency, security, and immutability to the ownership records.

3.   Investing in NFTs involves careful consideration of factors such as the creator's reputation, scarcity, utility, and demand within the market.

4.   NFT marketplaces are platforms where you can buy, sell, and trade NFTs. Each marketplace has its own features, fees, and community, so it's essential to research and choose the right platform for your needs.

5.   While NFTs offer tremendous potential for profit, it's crucial to be aware of the risks involved, including market volatility, scams, and copyright infringement issues.

6. Diversification, research, and staying informed about the latest trends and developments are essential strategies for successful NFT investing.

NEXT STEPS:

Further Education

As the NFT space continues to evolve, it's essential to stay updated on the latest developments, trends, and investment strategies. Follow industry news, subscribe to reputable blogs, and join online communities to connect with fellow enthusiasts and experts.

Attend Conferences and Webinars

Attend conferences, webinars, and workshops dedicated to NFTs and blockchain technology. These events often feature keynote speakers, panel discussions, and networking opportunities, providing valuable insights and connections.

Engage with NFT discussions, ask questions, and learn from experienced collectors and investors. Platforms like Discord and Telegram host vibrant communities where you can connect with like-minded individuals.

Explore NFT Marketplaces

Continuously explore various NFT marketplaces to familiarize yourself with different platforms and their offerings. This will help you understand the market dynamics and discover new investment opportunities.

Consider NFT Courses

Look for online courses and educational resources specifically designed to teach the fundamentals of NFT investing. These courses can provide structured learning experiences and insights from industry experts.

Connect with Creators

Engage with creators directly by following their social media channels or joining their communities. This will give you a deeper understanding of their work, upcoming releases, and potential investment opportunities.

Communities

Join online communities and forums dedicated to NFTs. Engage in Remember, NFT investing, like any form of investment, carries risks. It's crucial to exercise caution, conduct thorough research, and make informed decisions based on your financial goals and risk tolerance.

I hope this book has served as a valuable introduction to NFT investing and inspired you to explore this exciting new asset class further. Embrace the opportunities that NFTs present, and may your journey into the world of collectible digital assets be both rewarding and enlightening.

ABOUT THE AUTHOR

Usiere Uko

Usiere Uko is a writer, speaker and business and finance coach. Aside from running other businesses, he is involved in helping entrepreneurs grow their businesses and attain their potential through a faith-based business academy and empowerment programs.

Originally trained as a mechanical engineer with extensive experience in the oil industry spanning design, construction, project management and organisational capability, his passion has been to educate people to achieve their fullest potential and live fully through acquiring skills (especially financial skills) to enable them to achieve freedom in other areas of their lives as an integrated whole.

Among the publications he has written for includes Punch (AM Business) and Daily Trust (SME Business) Newspapers, Leadership & Lifestyle and Today's Lifeline magazines.

Usiere lives is happily married with a lovely son and daughter.

BOOKS IN THIS SERIES
SMART INVESTING 101

Money Market Investing 101: A Beginner's Guide To Low-Risk Short-Term Investments

Treasury Bill Investing 101: Your Essential Step-By-Step Guide To Building Financial Security

Treasury Bonds Investing 101: A Beginner's Guide To Low-Risk Investment Strategies

Treasury Notes Investing 101: Step-By-Step Guide And Smart Investor Starter's Handbook

Investing In Tips 101: A Beginner's Guide To Treasury Inflation-Protected Securities

Investing In Money Market Funds 101: The Beginner's Smart Investors Guide To Building Financial Security

Mutual Funds Investing 101: A Beginner's Guide To Building Wealth Through Smart Investing

Stock Market Investing 101: A Practical Beginners Guide To Online And Offline Stock Trading

Making Money With Life Insurance: Simple Strategies For Growing Wealth As A Beginner

Forex For Non-Traders: A Step-By-Step Guide To Earning Forex Income Without Trading

Investing In Peer-To-Peer Lending: A Beginner's Guide To Generating Passive Income Through Crowdlending Platforms

Investing In Etfs 101: A Beginner's Guide For Building Wealth With Exchange-Traded Funds

Nft Investing 101: A Beginner's Guide To Collectible Digital Assets

BOOKS BY THIS AUTHOR

Practical Steps To Financial Freedom & Independence

A Simple Guide To Investing In The Money Market

Before You Trade Forex

Before You Invest In Cryptocurrency

101 Common Money Mistakes To Avoid

How To Invest In Bonds

How To Invest In Treasury Bills (Bonds)

How To Avoid Living Under Financial Pressure

Financial Independence For Employees

Managing Your Money Post Covid

Retire On Your Own Terms

Your Ultimate Money Makeover

Teaching Kids Money 101

Uncle Ben's Money Lessons

www.ingramcontent.com/pod-product-compliance
Lightning Source LLC
LaVergne TN
LVHW051715050326
832903LV00032B/4207